REGIONS OF AMERICA

THE SOUTHWEST

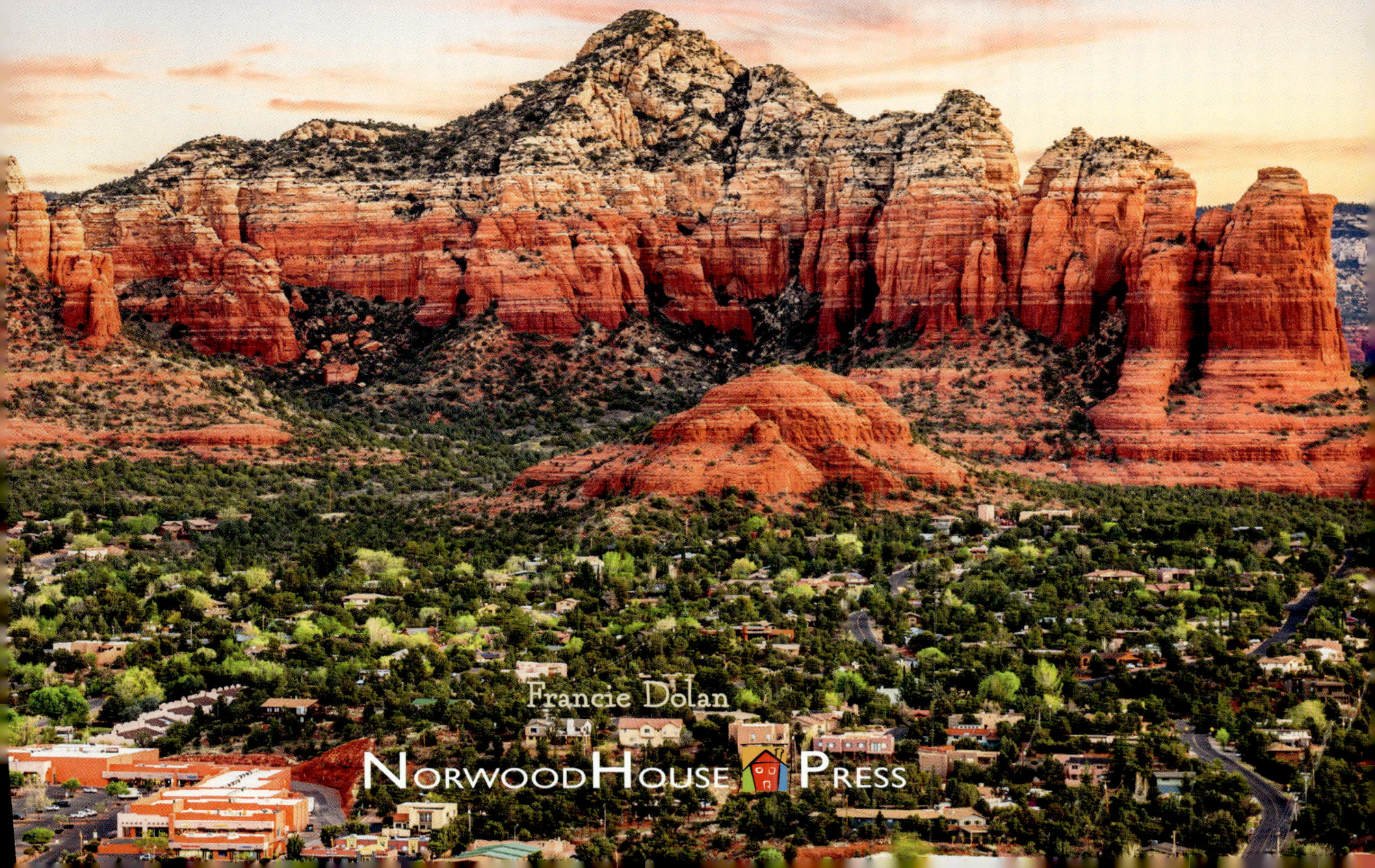

Francie Dolan

NorwoodHouse Press

Cataloging-in-Publication Data

Names: Dolan, Francie.
Title: The Southwest / Francie Dolan.
Description: Buffalo, NY : Norwood House Press, 2027. | Series: Regions of America | Includes glossary and index.
Identifiers: ISBN 9781978581258 (pbk.) | ISBN 9781978581265 (library bound) | ISBN 9781978581272 (ebook)
Subjects: LCSH: Southwestern States--Juvenile literature.
Classification: LCC F786.D65 2027 | DDC 976--dc23

Published in 2027 by
Norwood House Press
2544 Clinton Street
Buffalo, NY 14224

Designer: Rhea Magaro
Editor: Tricia Hoffman

Photo credits: Cover, p. 1 Sean Pavone/Shutterstock.com; p. 5 T photography/Shutterstock.com; p. 6 Grossinger/Shutterstock.com; p. 7 Brent Coulter/Shutterstock.com; p. 8 Keneva Photography/Shutterstock.com; p. 9 John Graybosch/Shutterstock.com; p. 10 LHBLLC/Shutterstock.com; p. 11 Evelyn D. Harrison/Shutterstock.com; p. 12 Library of Congress; p. 13 Andreas Stroh/Shutterstock.com; p. 14 G B Hart/Shutterstock.com; p. 15 Sean Pavone/Shutterstock.com; p. 17 Doug Meek/Shutterstock.com; p. 18 Sean Pavone/Shutterstock.com; p. 21 MICHAEL MCBRIDE AZ/Shutterstock.com;

Printed in the United States of America

CPSIA compliance information: Batch #CSNHP27: For further information contact Norwood House Press at 1-800-237-9932.

TABLE OF CONTENTS

WHERE IS THE SOUTHWEST?

The Southwest is a **region** of the United States. It has four states.

The Southwest

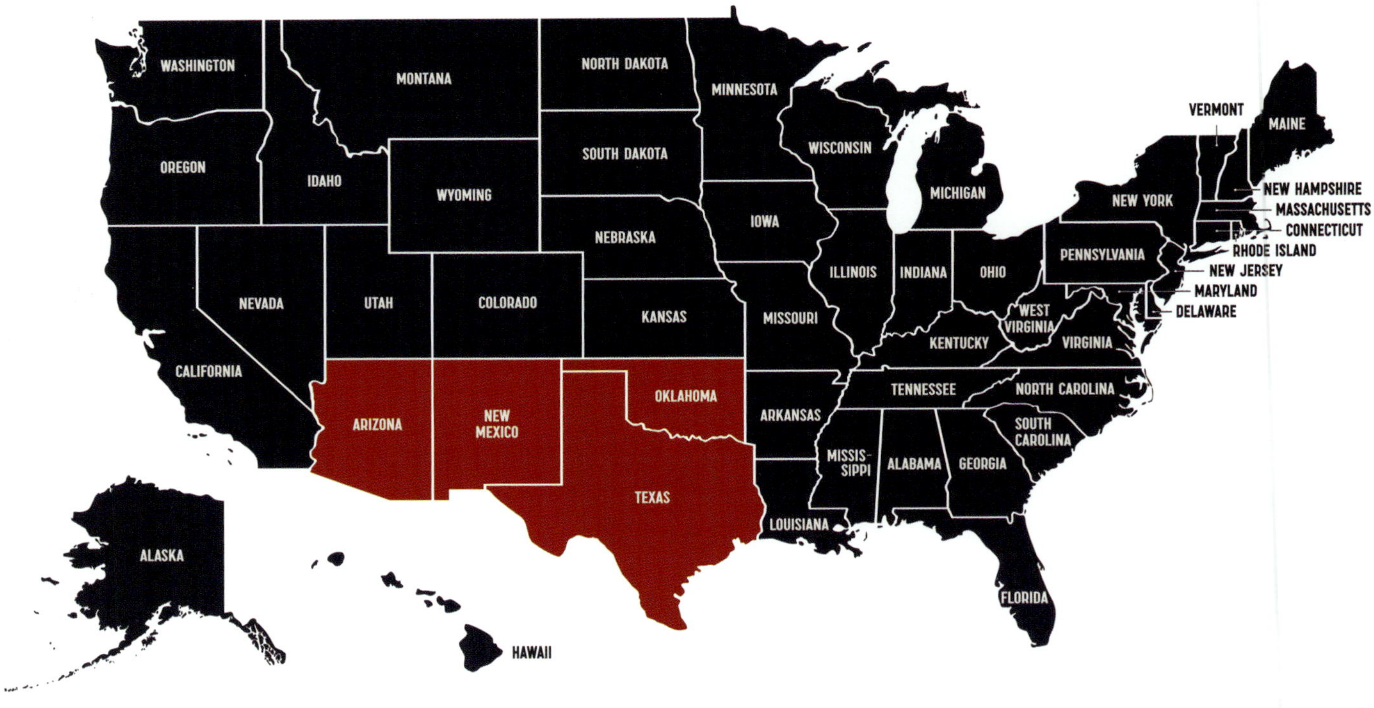

THE LAND

The Southwest is mostly south of the Rocky Mountains. It is west of the Mississippi River. All the states, except Oklahoma, border Mexico.

Most of the Southwest is **arid**. Some is **desert**.
It is rarely cold enough for snow.

Wind and water carve rock into special shapes. **Mesas** and **buttes** tower overhead.

Flowing rivers form deep **canyons**. One is the Grand Canyon in Arizona. It was created over millions of years by the Colorado River.

The Sonoran Desert reaches into Arizona. The Chihuahuan Desert is in Arizona, New Mexico, and Texas.

Deserts in the Southwest have **species** found nowhere else in the world. They include animals like the Gila monster and plants like the saguaro cactus.

THE PEOPLE

Indigenous people once lived across the region. Some tribes were the Navajo and Zuni.

Before it was part of America, the Southwest was controlled by Spain and then Mexico. Many people have Native American and Mexican **heritage**.

Many people live in small towns. Some work on ranches. Some drill for oil or work in mines.

Many people live in **urban** areas. Big cities include Phoenix, Arizona, and Houston, Texas.

THINGS TO SEE AND DO

In New Mexico, you can visit Carlsbad Caverns National Park. It has the Big Room. It is the largest cave chamber in North America. An elevator takes you down to it.

You can visit the Alamo in San Antonio, Texas. At this old fort, a group of Texans died in battle. They were trying to win freedom from Mexico.

Montezuma Castle is a special place in Arizona. Here, you can see an ancient cliff dwelling. Native people lived in it hundreds of years ago.

GLOSSARY

arid (AR-id): extremely dry because of a lack of rain

buttes (byoots): large, wide hills or mountains with steep sides and flat tops

canyons (KAN-yuhnz): deep, narrow river valleys with steep sides

desert (DEZ-urt): a place that gets less than 10 inches (25 centimeters) of rain each year

heritage (HER-i-tij): your background, including your family, country, culture, and beliefs

Indigenous (in-DI-juh-nuhs): the earliest known people to live in a place

mesas (MAY-suhz): skinny, tower-like hills with steep sides and flat tops

region (REE-juhn): an area or territory; part of a country

species (SPEE-sheez): a group of living things that are alike and can reproduce together

urban (UR-buhn): having to do with cities and city life

THINKING QUESTIONS

1. Name three states in the Southwest.
2. What Southwestern states touch Mexico?
3. Name a big city in the Southwest.
4. Name one Native American tribe from the Southwest.
5. What is the Alamo?

INDEX

ABOUT THE AUTHOR

Francie Dolan is a writer from Seattle, Washington. She loves American history and trivia. It is her goal to travel to all 50 states, visit their capital cities, and eat a special food from each place.